Hello There

Merle —

These are written by a village poet, but they certainly are not village poems — more of " emotion (NOT) recollected in tranquillity." (Wordsworth)

All Best,
U.D.

DeWitt
Village of Shorewood
12/13/21

Hello There

DeWitt Clinton

Word Poetry

Published by Word Poetry

P.O. Box 541106

Cincinnati, OH 45254-1106

ISBN: 9781625493927

Poetry Editor: Kevin Walzer

Business Editor: Lori Jareo

Visit us on the web at www.wordpoetrybooks.com

For all those who perished in the World Pandemic:

May their memories be a blessing.

Acknowledgments

Grateful acknowledgment is made to the editors of the following periodicals in which these poems were first published, sometimes in slightly different versions or different titles:

Across the Margin: "All Aboard," "On Hearing Another Poet Has Died"

American Writers Review 2021 - Turmoil and Recover: "Soon"

Anti-Heroin Chic: "The Way We Live," "What Is About to Happen Has Already Happened," "How Amazing," "Spin Cycle"

The Bezine: "Lazy Bums Vanish from Lazy Town," "Don't be Stupid," "So What Do You Do?"

Ekphrastic Review: "On Considering Winter Landscape with Ice Skaters," "Study Guide: The Fall of Icarus"

Fudoki Magazine {England}*: "Dust to Dust"*

Muddy River Poetry Review: "Did You Take the Trash Out, Dear?," "Hello There," "On Approaching a 70th Year," "So So Happiness," "Sun Burn," "Something, Something," "Keep Talking"

New Reader Review: "Instructions on the Way Out the Door," "Goodbye in Case I Have to Go"

New Verse News: "The Blood Has Stained Our Streets Something Bad"

One: "What Do You Think the Stars Are For?"

Poetry Hall: "On Hearing of So Many Dead"

Portage Magazine: "Life Without You"

Santa Fe Literary Review: "Losing Everything (Eventually)"

The Alterrian: "Aubade"

Verse-Virtual: "Interview with Rune," "Last Wishes," "Maureen's Gone and We'll Be Gone Soon, Too," "Our House," "Piano Lessons," "Please Stay," "Soldier to Soldier Outside the Church of the Nativity, Bethlehem," "How Long," "Just Wait"

Wisconsin Poets' Calendar 2021: "Pausing, Briefly, in a Moment of Fog"

Contents

III: Hello There

I: Our House

What Do You Think the Stars Are For?

We are all candles, aren't we, flickering away
Our lives so much we hardly have time to just

Pause, yet we do, even if some illuminate more
Of caved ceilings in the Pyrenees while some

Of us just look up from the fields of grain planted
Before we knew their names. Now we wander

In and out of houses, some plastered, some wood,
Some with the new iron of our age, some going

To the bathroom, some finding someone to spend
The night with, some planning away the future

As if it was there. But always we return to what
We think we'll be, or who we might have been,

Even Uncle Raphael's new painting in the Uffizi
Gives us all a moment to hold our breath. Still we

Do this, watching our lives flicker, wondering if we
Get to do this tomorrow. A few of us, including

Gertrude, don't want to go on this path, rather we'll
Just saunter down to the white sand beach, and ask,

How long can we stay, did you bring a book? Some
Of us will make others lunch, and some, so rude, will

Not even think about the service we've given, even
If it turns out the Greek salad needed a few more

Olives, a few more chunks of that sweet, white cubed
Milk we love to call feta. For some this is pretty much

It, as we are not ever going to get to go behind what
So many of us think is out there, beyond the stars.

Perhaps we can invent something that will make us
Wake up, even though the forecast is for more snow.

The Way We Live

Some still impress us with thick portfolios.
Some notice only the waxing moon.
If we look somewhere, we'll never see the breezes.
If we remember, we can't count all beneath us.

The Age of Terror may never end.
Fear keeps us texting whr r u?
Is there any place we haven't heard about?
On the Black Sea, none of us may eat.

I arrived crying, and still do.
I only laugh at the blue screen.
Every day, I hear judges,
Hope for any reduced sentence.

It's harder to know, for sure,
Unless your boot fills my breath.
Sure, everyone is a friend
But no one speaks anymore.

Don't be certain what you see.
Don't regret what's been whispered.
Go ahead, dream, but don't be scared.
Soon that's all we'll do.

Someday the rains will fall inside our homes.
Cold baths, day and night.
Then we'll escape to the roof
Only to see the sea, everywhere.

The axis will not change.
The clouds evaporate into Greek stars.
On our backs, clammy, we'll count how
Far away we are, knowing we're not there yet.

Pausing, Briefly, In A Moment of Fog

Yesterday, pushing up a hill, in fog, fog lights
Of drivers keeping me to the right, I hear
Behind me the lovely honking of visiting
Geese who fly along the coast line just
Below the fog. When they pass over
I turn and look up, careful to watch
For falling fecal matter that would
Ruin everything, so perfect, Canadians
On their way home, fog that keeps
All of us in silence, the hill that still
Needs to be ascended, and then
It all disappears and no moment
Like this will ever come by like the
Friend it has been, lonely, disappearing.

On Hearing of So Many Dead

Things are bad of course, as bad as ever, as bad
As any of us ever thought the world could be
But then sometimes I hear crickets or mourning doves
And wonder why they haven't disappeared from us.
Then I begin to think not everything is quite so bad
So I can without any fear open the back door and go
Down to the little creek that runs through our land
And listen carefully to what the owls already know,
And what the night life has for plans to keep on living.
I look up and see a huge yellow moon, hear the
Cracking of sticks as if something is moving somewhere
And nowhere do I think it's going to be bad, unless
Of course, something moves with such stealth that
I hardly notice when someone suddenly is not there.

Something, Something

We have to find stuff, everyday
Or we'll run out of stuff, everyday
But finding stuff with you that
Has made all the difference.
We need gas to go somewhere
We need food to keep going somehow
We need lots of prescriptions as
We're not as young as we'd like.
We don't need help yet going
Down the stairs, but pretty soon
One of us will probably hold
The other going up maybe down.
We do need each other's hands
To know we're just that far away.
We're okay on air though one
Of us got junky stuff down there
And had docs and nurses for days
And days, but that's all over now,
For now. We're salting less so
When we're out and something's
Salty, we talk a lot about the salt.
In company we try very hard not
To talk about what hurts, but then
Almost everyone is talking about
What hurts even if it's painful
Politics that makes us blab on so.
We still shampoo and shave as
The public view is still something
We don't ever want to forget just yet.
We're not into earth colors anymore
As we'll be earth colors soon enough.
One of us uses a walker and the other
Is learning how to race and walk but
We always arrive on the day someone

Thinks we're expected even if we're not.
We both have wondered why *not that*
Is something both of us can nod about.
We howl and howl over terrible dog &
Cat shows and wonder what's going on
With our constantly shrinking brains
That makes us curl up on the floor
Over some of the most idiotic scenes
But then we're glad really glad to be
Able to find a way to get ourselves
Back up and ready for something,
Of course, it doesn't really matter
So much anymore, as long as there's
Just something, something more.

Goodbye in Case I Have To Go

If I had to leave, immediately, unexpectedly,
As I have to go now, no time to even pack,
I'd want to say how much I enjoyed all
Of you, from top to bottom, every day, along
With everything else you've ever done, but
I did want to say, and don't take this like
You will, which you probably will, but
Next time, perhaps we should have more
Dogs and fewer cats, but that's just what
I've been thinking about as I am rushing
Out of the house, not even realizing that
I'm not going to be rushing out of the
House any more, ever, as I'm about to
Be exited, as someone might say, or
Dusted, or mowed down, or simply
Passed over, and now I'm even wondering
What the heck is passed over supposed
To mean, but then it doesn't really
Matter, does it, as this is it sweetheart,
And I only hope all those walks we took
Outside our little hotel in Florence or
Even on the beach in The Yucatan, well,
It was fun wasn't it? Of course, I have to
Go now, as I'm not even expected to know
What to expect, but something dreadful
Is going to happen and if it doesn't, I'll
Be forever grateful that I may have even
One more moment with you but that's
Asking way too much knowing what
May have already happened without
Even knowing what's already happened.
I know as this is probably a goodbye though
I really didn't mean forever, just until
Dinner, or drinks, sometime this evening.

What Is About to Happen Has Already Happened

Pleasant. Yes, that sounds about right. More pleasantness,
Please. After all, we'd all like each other more and more
If only we expressed more pleasantries, more cake,
As who really wants to sit and listen to a misanthrope
Go on and on about what a dreadful night it was.
Let's all hip hip hooray our way out of here with cheery
Thoughts so no one might ever imagine how awful what
Is about to happen has already happened, and no one
On my block is never ever going to talk about it, as
Just saying the word will make every one of us just
Start puking our guts out right at the curb knowing
Nobody, nobody is going to bother to wipe the mess
Up or at least away so it will stay there, drawing such
Big Blow Flies we've ever seen with a stink that makes
All of us going by just want to wretch on top of what's
Already there. And the blinding Sun only makes it hard
& finite, like it's never going to leave and then by luck
A bird so light lands and starts gobbling up all
The nutrients, all the tiny seeds, all the slivers, all of
What came up and out, so even now, it's starting to
Look a little brighter here, a bit sunnier, and someone
Just now took a breath, and smiled, yes, it's very
Possible if rains should come it will all be pleasant,
Again.

Lazy Bums Vanish from Lazy Town

"Once upon a time there was a town where all the
people were exceedingly lazy."
—The Lazy Townspeople

It's true of course as we all know those
Lazy folks just down the road will do
Just about anything to not do just about
Anything, hoping some nincompoop

Will show up just in time to rake up
All the trash, bag it, maybe recycle it,
And send all that is not wanted on its
Merry way. When even that didn't

Work out, the old folks were just beside
Themselves to get themselves going
So the place might look a bit more
Spiffy when the man in the white house

Who now owns everything and everyone
Will drive by for a view, and toss a few
Coins to those whose waving hands
Are the highest ever for free handouts.

That was at least the plan. The old town
Though just got older, stinkier, trashier,
And big bugs soon arrived by the millions
So no one could get a night's rest without

Bites everywhere and anywhere but as
You know, no one knew quite what to do.
We could all make rakes, a ratty man said.
I've got a bunch of mowers, said the long

Beard. The smelly old one even kept empty
Bottles of Clorox and Windex just in case.
Everybody said let's get started, but no
One really started, as no one had ever

Known how to bring spring to the old town.
A well-kept girl crawled under the hedge
That kept those in and those looking out
And she knew right away what might spif

The place up, shiny and brassy as before.
Follow me, she said, and everybody did
Just that, and soon the town was not ever
There, no one could even remember it,

And then, what nature does best, a big
Wind came through and the wind coughed
It all around the world as it was most
Disgusting with all the dust, and mites,

And those terrible bugs that get into
Everything, and soon the man in the
Big white house drove down to see
His priceless town, and it was so shiny,

Smooth, and not a trace could be found
Of the terrible people who once called
What once was trash, what once was home,
A fine place to wave his tiny, clean hands.

Dust To Dust

Adapted from the Chinese myth, Houyi and Chang'e,
the Goddess of the Moon

i

Even before time or once
Upon a time or even
Before long ago
Heaven ruled ten unruly sons
Making this place a moonscape.
Only moon dust flowered
All over the planet, in the
Oceans, in the forests,
Even in the coldest bear caves.

Time's up said Heaven
And sent out a contract
On those hotheaded ten.
And Heaven sent Houyi, earth's archer,
Who looked into the sky
Blazing with ten suns.
One by one each turned
Into star dust leaving one
Sun to keep the earth
From turning into all Iceland.

But Heaven mourned what
Turned her sons into
Distant star dust
And banned Houyi and goddess
Chang'e from Heaven, to live
Out their days in a burned out
Hard as stone earth garden.

ii

The archer and his wife found
Life on earth too miserable
To stay as they soon saw how
Each was turning older and
Older and would soon turn
As others do into dust.

Then Houyi remembered his
Queen Mother who lived
The high life here on earth
Who kept what Houyi wanted,
A few sips of a honey-laced
Elixir for the two honeymooners.

High on Mount Kunlun
Queen Mother listened to
Houyi, deliberating, of course
The what if's he could
Not ever imagine might happen.

Half of this nectar is all you
May take to stay here and live
Out all your days and nights
Forever and forever.   If

However you both are induced
With all of the elixir, you will
Lose this life, return to Heaven,
And live as you once lived,
Forever in immortality.

Houyi, exhausted but relieved,
Rested in the arms of Chang'e
Until he fell into a deep sleep.
Curious, she felt drawn
To a life of a better life

Living to see everything
Always, forever, here
As one of the only immortals.

iii

So she drank the whole portion
Forgetting of course Houyi's
Hope of living out this life
As well, forever and forever.

Soon she fell into a deep sleep,
Began to feel weightless,
Began to float away,
Forever and forever.

But she did not float to Heaven,
She did not float back to Earth, either,
But found the Moon, and on the Moon
She lived the life of a goddess,
Doing whatever immortals do
In her Palace with her only
Company the quiet Jade Rabbit.

Upon waking, Houyi knew what
His lovely Chang'e had turned
Into, and Houyi lived out the rest
Of his days, hoeing the earth,
Turning in age, turning into dust.

In the Autumn we turn our eyes
To the Moon, and remember
Where one immortal may still be
Stepping, forever, into moon dust.

Interview with Rune

Where do most (poems) grow?
    Under hate or injustice
Or regrettably in the tumbling
    Of love and death.

How do they ignite the world?
    In the far recesses
    Of sleep.

Can any ever move a stone?
    Once in Ireland we've heard
This, & of course, whenever
    We hear this, we wonder more.

We've heard some lie in wait
    For countless years. How
Can this be true? Few are ever
    Present when the two are one.

Some have tried counting all
    Of the many. Is this wise?
No one here has ever
    Quantified such madness.

When some fall asleep why do so
    Many rhyme in triplets?
Some who dream see this
    As the only desires left.

Why do so many appear when
    One or two begin to walk?
We've heard this also by some
    Who swim near the bottoms.

Most stay in inner recesses when
    Not in use. Why is this?
For if not there, where
    Could anyone feel safe?

We've not seen odes to fallen soldiers
    In quite some time. Can you tell us more?
So many have died since the first wars, few
    Notice the losses & stones in neat rows
    Replace what once was sorrow.

Birds have sometimes been thought
    To hold the last stanzas.
Yes & in the howling winds.

Do they ever seek their own solace
    As we do?
Unfortunately, no.
    Their only salvation is being found.

Study Guide: "The Fall of Icarus" for Ms. Hansen's English 9 Power Slide 7

What is the subject of the painting? (Hint It is not Icarus)

I like the ploughman's head pointed
Down to earth just like his horse looks
Down to see where to step. Everybody
Says look up, lift your gaze, look ahead,
See what's going on when ploughing
The earth up for spring planting.
If he doesn't look down he won't see
A big old rock that might bust his blade,
And then what's the horse good for?
I like the plowman's shirt.

List what the various people (ploughman, shepherd, fisherman, crew) are doing.

They're all going about their business,
Though I don't know much about the
Businesses. Haven't you noticed,
Nobody notices what everybody
Else is doing isn't that what we notice?

Identify the event that is going unnoticed.

The guy with the red head who points.
He's not about to jump into and save
The poor nincompoop, he just wants to point,
Like the guy who says I'm just a monitor,
He's the monitor who sees a boy falling,
With wings of hot wax and charcoal feathers.
But maybe he just sees two legs in the ocean.
The other day I read about a body pulled
Out of the lake and nobody helped him out.

29

Other than his father, Daedalus, who will mourn Icarus? Base
your answer on evidence in the painting, not conjecture.

As soon as that leg sinks below
Everybody's going to turn around
And just keep on doing what
They were doing before the
Big tragedy, though no one
Really thinks it's a big tragedy.
Maybe even the painter didn't
Think it was such a big tragedy,
Maybe he just had some extra
Red paint he wanted to get off
Of his brush. Who really knows?

Based on the evidence in the painting, what is the artist's view,
or attitude, about Icarus falling to his death?

Well, a lot more things are noticed
By the artist, for example he likes
White cliffs, and white clouds, and
White sunlight, and white sails and
White sheep and white shirts and
White towns but he did a pretty
Good job with a couple of dabs
Of red. Where did he get that red?

On Considering "Winter Landscape with Ice Skaters," Hendrick Avedrcamp, c. 1608.

Oil on Panel

We're pretty much done with winter here
Though today the rain showers have turned
The whole place into an ice palace no one
Really appreciates unless one has the luxury
Of looking outside from the inside where
Almost all of us are, at this moment, taking
Note of the few skaters outside without
Skates, some leaving earth for only a brief
Time, then returning without having seen
Any of the heavens, just a slight slip that
Takes the whole body out of what keeps
Us all grounded until we step on the patch
That will catch so many unscheduled lifts
Only to be returned briefly, a second later,
Arriving not upright but at a slant, not feet
Landing as we are accustomed to, but our
Already sore back will be the first to reach
Earth, and none will consider any laws of
Gravity that keeps us here, and not up
There, but soon, we will watch the skaters
Attempting to regain poise as the feet
Slip on even more of the place no one
Should place a foot, but then, this is
Where we are, for now, and then we turn
To the kitchen to warm up what's left
Of homemade soup, and warm bread,
And pretend that it's really no different
Than any skater who looks out on a
Medieval pond seeing those who are
Gliding, and those, sadly, who are not.

Our House

Our house is a large containment unit for burglars, rapists, murderers, car thieves, and so many who have assault records. It's hard to know any more where to bed them down every night, but we do march them into a tiny little box of pixels where they won't hurt anyone or at least we hope so. We give them crackers and cheese to make it through the night.

Our house is a small chain of on-line clothing and warehouse fashion items of tops, and dresses and sweaters, and pants, and T-shirts, and jammies, and coats and gloves and scarves and boots and way too many shoes, and underwear.

Our house is an ever-changing grocery aisle of foods from all nations, kept frozen in the kitchen or in the basement, or in the pantry or in the icebox, or out on the counters for easy reach. Recyclables always go in the big black bag out back.

At night, in our house, and sometimes in the late afternoons, we entertain ambassadors, emissaries, presidents, speakers of houses, chairs of committees, all representatives of all foreign governments who visit us (and complain a lot) over the waves of pixels. Breaking news always comes into our house with exciting music.

In our bedroom, we've hosted extraterrestrials, big bad bugs, bacteria, bomb blasts, just about everything that goes gooey if stepped on or smashed but we have spray cans to defend ourselves from big green flies if any try to break through the tinty screen. One flick of the remote and all vanish. In our house we are always looking out the windows after Scully and Mulder scare away the aliens.

In our house, we have laundry that goes down the chute, and miraculously, is washed and folded and brought back up in large baskets, gifts from the basement that never cease to amaze us.

Inside our house, we have cooling agents. We have heating agents. We have cold water agents and hot water agents, and by another miracle the blinds are closed at sundown and are open for the next sunrise, something of a miracle in our little house.

Outside our house grass grows both in the front and in the back, and flowers bloom and cherry tomatoes never cease to appear, though we wonder who might be tending to these mysterious tasks.

Stars and goddesses visit our house again and again, as we like their scripts even though we know what's going to happen, and even if we don't, it's always a delight to see them in pixels. We sometimes see their *oeuvre* in an encore performance, but that's when both of us are insomniacs.

Messages from afar always arrive at our house, sometimes encoded with payment for services for services sometimes we wonder about. We send all that we've created out for review and most of it comes back for us to review again.

In our house, we have dozens of paintings some even under glass, but our viewing hours are quite limited as we are open for viewing so seldom anymore.

Outside our house we see an Escape which takes us to all of our appointments and reservations, and the chauffeur is quite pleasant, most of the days.

In our house, when someone asks what's for dinner, in an hour or less, dinner arrives, and we are most impressed by the cutlery, the china, and always, what's on the china. The butler always chooses something we've tried before. The frozen dinners are always so tasty. We are most amazed at this miracle of miracles.

In our house, we sometimes stand behind a clear curtain, and warm water from unknown sources sprays us down and up, and we are so refreshed after. We look forward to the next time for this localized rain shower.

In our house, one of us is always yelling to the other of us as our intercom has never existed, so we have to throw our voices long distances in order to have a favor completed.

In our house, we look outside and see all the seasons, and somebody always arrives to blow away the leaves, or pick up and toss the snow and ice, so we don't fall down and break more bones.

In our house, sometimes someone is on the floor, and white coats always arrive to take a pulse, and then one of us appears in front of doctors and nurses and sometimes we stay in a house with many others like us, and when better, we always come back to our house.

We've decided to stay in our house, for now, unless the aliens crowd us out and start snacking on our limbs. We've had this problem before in other houses, and we have always learned to be calm and gracious before we disappear.

In our backyard, out back, we have planted our dead pets, and we've started to wonder if there's any room left under the daylilies in case one or both of us is still in our house, and has left for good.

If there's time, when we're not in our house anymore, please read and see and enjoy and taste everything in the house, before you throw it all out for the wolves and ravens who will have their own say about what went on here, in this house, where we lived for two centuries, almost.

II: Instructions On the Way Out The Door

Losing Everything (Eventually)

"The art of losing isn't hard to master."
Elizabeth Bishop

I wish I knew what's going on, or gone,
As I can't quite remember what I'm

Doing here with you but I wanted
Very much to just drop by but

Now I wonder just why I left
The house for something so simple

As a coffee and a bagel and there
I'm standing at the counter wondering

Where's my billfold or even cash
Driving home a back route to stay

Out of range of waiting patrol cars
That just might stop me as I look

Just like that old guy out for a drive
Without his wallet or even a wad of cash

But it's worse you see just yesterday
I left a satchel full of old snails, shells

And only later knew I'd left them
On their own in the quiet dark.

It's been like this for days and days
I can't remember how many days of

Losing keys, forgetting cash, leaving
Paper and pen in places I never should,

But then I'm quite relieved knowing
How I'll lose a lot more than just

These, or maybe not just lose, but
Forget that I'd better be here with than

Without, but it's true I'm also losing
Height, down an inch, and can't see

All the way back to the back of a
Room I'm in, or grey cells which

Seem to be absent without any
Thank you or permission for leave,

Or friends who I can't quite figure
Out why they aren't around or

The time it used to take to run
A race, but for now let's not

Appreciate the art of losing things
As Elizabeth made so beautiful as

Losing is a lot worse than wandering
Around looking for more that's missing.

On Approaching a 70th Year

So it's been strange and delightful, mostly surprising
But anything anyone has ever done then or even *when*
Mostly ends up as something fabricated, but a good story.
I could try a glass of cold Pinot Grigio, but I'd like to keep
The sugars low, as no need to get another diagnosis unless
That's the only new one this year, but soon others will start
Gnawing their way up the system, and perhaps a little faster
Now that I'm on a short-term warranty, with no recent call ups
For used parts, or at least none are for sale or even available.
But there's also something good about turning this year,
That I'm still here, consuming resources, leaving deposits,
Filling a mind up with whatever schemes I can find that
Might help figure out what kind of world I'm still living in.
I'm trying to sit up more, lifting the sternum, as my yoga
Teacher usually always says when she sees my rounded
Shoulders nearly touching the floor, but then it's just crazy
To be upside down blood cleansing the old brain, or wrapped
Like a pretzel, remembering to keep the breath coming
In and letting a bit of it out, but not in any great burst
Like all the beefy guys at the gym do before a big lift.
What else? Friends, I do miss those who haven't stayed
Around, but they all wanted to, just couldn't figure how.
And father and mother, well, they've been gone some
Time now, and don't expect to see them unless I drive
Down to Carolina where they are buried, oddly, on top
Of each other. That's probably the only time ever they've
Been that close to each other, but the thought is still
Perturbing, but then, lots of folks lately have sort of
Gotten on my nerves, but I'm learning not to make too
Much of what anybody says, or thinks, or acts, anymore.
Those ahead of me suggest I'll soon start appreciating
Everything much more, even trips to the bathroom,
And sometimes, I can really appreciate their meaning.
I'm looking forward to some of this, whatever is about

To be what is, and have put off wondering what I'll be
Doing even tomorrow, as whatever is tomorrow won't
Quite be like what I expect it to be today, but who knows?
There's more of course, life insurance, prescriptions,
Power of attorney forms to fill out just in case something
Goes wrong, and everybody, everybody says whatever
You've got, it'll get worse, but even though I haven't
Seen all the places in the world I'd hope to see, still
It's not bad from this view, and hope the evenings will
Continue without too much drama, as I'd rather buy
Tickets for such occasions, than have them in my head.
Tomorrow's almost here, with cake and bubbly, so if
You want to stay on the list, pack a bag and stop by.

Did You Say Something, Dear?

There's a silence inside, and sometimes it's just too much
Though I'm not sure any of us know how to pry open what's
Been locked up for so very long, in fact, no one around here
Has any idea of what actually *was* locked up, or even where
It now might be, but it seems to float in and out of our minds
And always, one of us asks if the other knows where all that
Silence has been, but then, we hesitate as that'd be the start
Of something we haven't sensed in such a long time, questions
Framed in such a way to draw us out, when we've been out
For such a long time, but hasn't this happened to you as well,
Or are you sitting where you are, or maybe even dozing,
Wondering just the very same thing, and actually stopped
What was going on like chattering monkeys for so very long,
Then it was gone, like something we really never had much
Hold on, and now, now we're just drifting down a river that's
Way too wide to jump in and start swimming toward the edge
As now I can even feel the current moving much further
Along in the wrong direction, but perhaps that's where we're
Going, even if we don't want to be going in that direction,
And of course, this makes sense to you, doesn't it, for isn't
This something you've been working for most of your life
As well, but maybe not, as we're all so different, and most
Everyone these days is talking so much about so many in-
Consequential drifting thoughts that nobody, nobody really
Knows what anybody's really saying any more, but then,
No one really cares about that anymore, do they, or do they?

Tea

for Herman (1905-1995) Berta (1904-1997)
and Gunther Weil (1937-)

I tell my friend
Over and over
So many times
Over I wonder
Whether or not he even
Hears what I want him to say

Tell me what happened, tell me.

My old friend won't tell
What he knows but
What if I lived
Inside a cage
Buried somewhere
In Vietnam,
A place no one would find,
And then, let go
Just like that
Would I tell what I know
Just because someone
Wanted to know?

All I see is my old friend
Younger than even
I am now   French   with papers
From Alsace-Lorraine
Dressed in classic
Black and gray stripes
On his way home
Through a forest
Of faith alone

A reprieve
A constant mantra of *S'hma Yisrael*
Mortified of another arrest
Yet he has walked away
"On a technicality
Of birth," he says,
From a place called Buchenwald.

So what happened? I asked
But all he says
Is that he will not
Relive he will not
Say what he has
Not said for so long.

In Washington, D.C., I stand
In front of a museum glass case
Watching morning roll call
In sunny, cold Buchenwald
Everyone out bright and early
Achtung filling the only
Silence, and I press
Into the glass, looking
For my old friend.

Am I watching you?
Never considering
Even turning just slightly
To look up and see
Behind the glass
Me looking in
Some 60 years later.

In the next photograph
All I hear is the shuffle
Of American tourists
No one comes to stand
With me or

Even beside me
Even the dogs in the picture
Have gone
All that is left
Is a *minyan* of ten fine men
Swinging in the cold air
Why am I here looking in
Old friend &
Not looking out at you
What did these men do
That I have not done myself?

Instead my old friend tells
How his wife saved
His life how after
Endless trips to Nazi Offices
With warnings *Juden verboten*
Discouraging the boldest
She walks right in
Tells a desk sergeant
Her story of a French
Boy wrongly imprisoned

And then
There is nothing more
Anyone can do but wait
Nothing to do but weep
Weeks later my old friend
Walks away from Buchenwald
Smelling fir trees
Hearing song birds
Wearing black & white stripes
Holding his breath
So no one would again
Arrest him like that
Again.

My old friend

Sighs when he says
How breathless
He was when he knocked
On the door of his home
How the two lovers —
My old friend, his wife —
Couldn't stop crying
And in only hours
How they and their child
Sailed out of Bremen
Where I, too, once stood
Waving goodbye
Long after you left,
This time, on holiday,
After serving on tour
As private first class
In South Vietnam.

Last autumn the elderly
Couple invite the two
Of us over for tea
And dessert each
Of us mesmerized
What we can't tell
How impossible
To believe we were
Not there
Why we are
Here brought back
From the dead
Absorbed
In the place we all
Want to call home.

Soldier To Soldier Outside the Church of the Nativity, Bethlehem

Where Arabs hawk postcards,
And tired pilgrims rest
After prayers to the Christ child,
I walk over to a soldier
Who dozes in the Bethlehem heat,
Ask if his rifle is an M16.

He's surprised a tourist
Would know such things.
I tell him I carried
A rifle like his
Outside Chu Lai
In the Song Chang River Valley,
Words I've never wanted to say
Except now, with this kid.

He looks at me to make sure.
Did I shoot any VC?
Did I walk the boonies?
Did I get any poontang?
Then something he said,
As if his lips, tongue,
Teeth, throat moved into slow motion
Like tracers drawing a bead
On the enemy—

You're a hero, he says.

Not really, I try to tell him.
He says Yes, Yes, you're a hero,
And he smiles, happy to stand next to one,
Happy to tell his mother,
Everyone at dinner tonight,

Who he met today
Outside the Church of the Nativity.

What does he know
Of the battalion of NVA,
Slaughtered with seven batteries
Of heavy ground artillery,
A crap shoot, Capt. Willis bragged,
A fucking crap shoot,
We waited and waited
And waited all fucking afternoon
No one had ever
Seen that many gooks in the open before.

Another pilgrim in our tour steps
Into the bright piazza,
Wonders whatever in the world
Could we be talking about,
Walks over, asks to shoot
A picture of both of us,
One soldier standing next to a hero.

His weapon is in lock and load.
The boy soldier will protect us
From liberators, bombs, random stabbings,
Even a stone thrown over a Wall.
Next to him, I smell the stench
All over again,
Round after round
Pummeling good soldiers
Into the soft Asian ground.

I smile for a close up.
He welcomes me home,
My very own parade
My very own hero's parade.

A few others in our tour

Want a picture, too,
A victory parade
Here on this tour of the Holy Land
Lucky, fucking lucky,
To still have arms, legs,
The summer heat
Rising like the stench
Of all those boys
Their bones lost and forgotten
Revived with pilgrimages
Back to downed planes
Rusting metal parts
Quick easy graves
For the useless dead
Who always come back
On occasions
Where small crowds
Gather for honor and glory.

An Afternoon with Pi SSu Yao Who Visits Tu Fu in the 8th C.

It's quite questionable that we
Have any talent, but a few over
There in the clearing think so,
And perhaps that's enough, yes?
I've never wanted to lead anyone
Ever, except quickly in the moonlight
Hurrying away from an overrun
Bunker where N.V.A. soldiers
Follow right behind us ending
All we've ever dreamed about.
As to those houses, none have
Been that special, though I've
Enjoyed each one, somewhat,
And I've done most of my chores
In each one, and each house
Was clean when we left.
I secretly wish more of those
Editors would look over what
I've given them again, but
They're in a hurry, I know,
And I hurry as well to send
All of them out into the air
Again. No, we've not kept
Servants, ever, but if we did,
We'd clean right alongside
Just to make it easier for all.
O yes, more wrinkles, more
Squinty eyes, more crow's
Feet, more old yellowy nails.
Does anyone care about those
Old yellowy nails? Only the
Chatty old woman who washes
And trims away all the old

Relics, and more. We can
Keep an audience, of course,
But few of us really want
To listen. Is that true for
You? I know a few poets
All with immense stature,
At least for today. We'll
Be handed down, I expect,
But down exactly where,
Perhaps to an old book
Stall all on sale for so little.
But I am so relieved you
Are here. I'd be so forlorn
If I were just here with me. No, no
I'm pretty sure no one will make
A memory of this, and soon, both
Of us will be shorter, closer to
The ground beneath us. Any
Relative of yours will probably
See all of it, and throw all of it
Into the wind, just like we hoped.

Aubade

A day like this,
Who would have thought we would wake,
Think of ourselves as lucky to still be around?

After the thunderstorm, all I want
Is the fresh wet earth, the tiny
Tomatoes we can eat all at once.

Crows, outside our house, will never leave us.
As we unpacked, Harry says to Grace,
Watch them, never let them think
They can throw us out.

When I breathe, why think of anything?
Why would anyone want anything, say, today?

The field of napalm, mostly it's gone
Forever, but when I think of it,
I remember how the bombs
Floated so gracefully
Before everything shuddered,
And I was miles away,
Holding binoculars.
Am I still the one,
Sweating in a flak jacket?

When is it that I will feel
The opening of a rose, or you?

This day, all I see is the light filling
Our little room, thinking
All of it, all of it
Is a particle of then, and this.

Life Without You

Once on the other side,
No more "hello, dear"
To hear "hello."

There'd be the cat, of course, and maybe
Another one, just to make a home
With two instead of one.

What will I do with all these clothes,
All of them hanging downstairs
Each perfumed with you.

Everywhere there'd be you, in all
The rooms, things you'd have
Done all these years.

The sheets, who would decide
The color of the sheets this week?
That was always up to you.

Maybe I'd sleep more, no more
Up and down, old boards
Creaking through the night.

All those saved TV shows.
Who wants to see all those
Murderers show up again?

Maybe I'll take some
Of the blue ones.
What do the blue ones do?

There's a drawer full of underwear.
There's more downstairs.

Some just arrived in the mail.

If I could have nothing
Then maybe I'll just look
At your diamond ring.

No trips to the burial
Grounds. Been there
Once, that's enough.

Maybe I'll rent a
Movie. No need to whisper
If you're not here.

Maybe I'll just start
To walk, maybe I can
Walk all the way to work.

You're right, I'll start
Dusting, maybe the
Blue sheets will do.

Piano Lessons

Listening to gypsy jazz one cool morning
I'm reminded of those terrible off to school
Piano lessons, scales, and bad Beethoven

As a grade school kid under the scornful
Eye of Mother who now I'm not convinced
Ever played the keys herself thinking it

Wasn't Mother who needed the lessons but
A child who will make something of himself
If only he can catch the click of the metronome

Every once in a while singing the notes of
Dah da da da da Da da da Dahh da da da da
Da da da hmmmm hmmmm hmmmm hmmmm

Then slipping into the noose of a baby tuba
And band practice, and pretending to play
The piccolo at the homecoming parade

But voice seemed more and more a possibility
First in choir, then a cappella, double choir,
Choir tours through the state, a few solos

Long before anyone thought of American Idol
But now I neither sing nor play much to the
Dismay of Mother who wanted a musician

Out of her little grade-schooler, but instead,
Whenever Sam starts singing "A Kiss is Just a Kiss"
In *Casablanca*, I always join in knowing no one

Will hear an old crooner, a little off key,
Out of practice, happy just to be off camera,
A little misty eyed, still looking for lovely Ilsa.

How Amazing

Sometimes before the grey sets in
Before the late afternoon quietly
Eases down and the doves lament
Whatever has not yet been
It's then that I wonder, like Mother,
How many more of these days
Anyone keeps together as one comes
And then another and then another
And pretty soon, one can't remember
Anything anybody's ever done so
Why does it take so long to just
Finish what we started, but most
Of us don't have any idea what
That was, or even anything that was,
Perhaps that's it, we're just here to
Keep everything moving until one
Forgets what there is to move,
So now all we're able to do is
So simple just count the dust that
Floats forever by us in such thin light
And it's then we know nothing
Really is quite what we say it is
Even if we all say How Amazing.

Like a Plum

Or a walnut which makes more sense
But of course, softer like a plum within
Reach of the yearly exam with palms
Gripping the paper towel table a
Slicked up forefinger going in ever
So reluctantly the sounds coming
Out of the mouth most unusual, tearful
Even if one could call it that, then of
Course the raise your shorts talk
Along with a few sheets of hankies
To take care of the greased anus
Not to forget the peeing into a very
Tiny jar with your name wrapped
Around the sides so as to not get
Mixed up with more bleak situations
And if there's not much leaking out
Then a lie down exam with cold gel
Right on top the bladder to just see
Underneath how much did not find
The route to the exit and on out in
Open air trickling into a large bowl
Then another door where a white
Coat draws a rubber wrap around
Your elbow and smiles saying smile
As a needle enters a vein looking
For elevations above acceptable
With a urologist's signature at
The bottom of a script indicating
Once again the magical powers
Of little white pills which in weeks
Could bring the numbers down
Until it's finally time to go in
In an unexpected entrance to
Scrape away or down until just

A miniature of the plum or even
More a shrunken walnut no longer
Sending out jet streams, but
Luckily, letting the flow return
As it once did long before this.

Dreaming of Who I Am Not

(After Billy Collins' "One Self")

If I were someone who I am not
Maybe I'd be someone who
I would never have known
Maybe that would be even better

Even if I could imagine myself
As someone who I am not
The idea of being there
And not over here

Is way beyond anything
I might want to try on my own,
Yet the possibility of being who
I am not is a lovely thought

For then I could become all
Those big bellied baritones who
Sing with a scarf and break
Hearts all throughout Europe

And various whereabouts,
And then I could look out
Into the darkened balconies
And see myself about to

Join me in a final chorus of arias
Only I know better for it's
Quite a leap from there to here
& the fall through the lights

Would leave everyone sore
Ruining all the crescendos
All the sopranos leaving everyone

In much more than a final reprieve

Maybe an aria, a duet, so the
DeWitt I am might be better
employed just dreaming of
The Met or the Lyric or some

Polish opera house I keep going
Back to in all my travels through
All the worst death and ashes ever
Found near such lovely places

As Warsaw or Lublin or Krakow
So for now, I can turn up the
Medley of arias and solos in
My Focus, roll down the window

Letting all of these creatures
Both winged and four-footed
Hear what they're missing and though
Father and Mother are buried far

Away in some sweet little town
Way down in the South, I hope that
By now I will be able to get through
La Traviata without thinking of you.

Young David

You'd think by now we'd know how
To whirl a stone around and around
Until we learn how to just let go
And see what might happen if
Anything happens when a stone
Meets the furrowed brow of
Someone so big with such a big head
Surely no one could make someone
Fall down like that, but I've learned
Since the early dawn show-down
That we never tire of throwing
Something at someone we don't
Want to have anything to do
With even if the other is such
A nincompoop anybody would
Know that a frightened flock
Of sheep could topple even
The tallest of our enemies
We'd like to see fall down
And stay down but in fact
Our enemies always appear
Just over the crest asking
For more land, more space,
More women, more goats
If we have goats in fact
More of everything is what
A loudmouth-with-tiny-hands
Bully wants but keep in mind
Centuries later a little star fleet
Fighter named Luke will bring
Down the biggest ball of all
Slinging a terrible boom-boom
Into the whirling Death Star
So once again most of us

Can rest awhile until the next
Goliath finds what he wants.

The Blood Has Stained Our Streets Something Bad

Something is out there, and we're all just a bit
Terrified of what's going to happen next, but
What in the heck can we do about something
That we can't even see when it's coming about
To slash and twist us about so turning us into
Just about everything we've never ever wanted
To be, or even not be, and it's just awful the way
Some of us know that it's pretty hard to stop
What we don't want, or grab at what we do
By crying out loud, or even whispering, but
Some suggest we find all our sleeping masks
And look around in the kitchen for kitchen knives
And run outside in the dark which is darker
Than we've ever known, but now we're slashing
And stabbing and hoping one of those we
Think we're gutting will be what's started us
All into the panic we're in, even on such a
Cold night in the smack dab middle of March
And we don't want to make too much of it
But we do go out in the morning to see if any
Can find any blood splatters, anything that
Might let us know we've once again shaken
The cry baby who keeps us all up late at night,
Twittering and tweeting scaring the whatever
Out of us, but now we can rest a bit until the
Next blowhard makes a mess of something
Out there, which is really here, where we are.

Did You Take the Trash Out, Dear?

It's late, as you know, or may not know
Though you may have a few extra
Minutes before lights are turned out
For all of us, but I seem to remember
So many light bulbs are burning out
Faster than I can find the step ladder
To step up into the next layer of light
To make the tricky turns so as to
Not separate the bulb from the screwy
As I've done this and find I'm now down
In the basement with flashlight looking
At the updated fuse box to see which
Has flipped, even slightly flipped for
These days unless you're the expert
It's harder and harder to tell, but that's
Not really why we're here, is it,
As I've sensed everything important
Is slowing down, but please don't
Call anyone as that'd be embarrassing
But don't you, too, feel something is
Just not right anymore, as the light
Seems to be dimming all around
Not just in our little brick house
Which has ample lighting, of course,
But I'll admit I'm walking slower
Than I have and when I do, I sense
A slight tilting or drifting as it's hard
To stay on that fine line, looking a bit
Screwy like I've had too much to drink
Which might be true, but then
The zigging and zagging of walking
Down the block happens even without
Evening refreshments, and another
Thing that's odd is that the plates

Are a bit smaller than they used
To be and I've no problem with
That just that the appetite is like
The smaller plate, and we've even
Gone to plastic spoons, why I'm
Not sure, but the wife says they're
Pretty, aren't they, and I do agree
But there's something out there,
Don't you see it, too, that's making
Everything a bit dimmer, duller
Or perhaps it's just that time
Of the year when all the snow
Has turned to a dirty grey pile
But I'm quite optimistic not
About any of this, but just pressing
The old nose up close to something
Even if it is sniffing out what's what
As in what's that yet I don't remember
That being there, wasn't it over
There, but maybe these things
Don't ever bother you, and they
Don't exactly bother me, but there's
Just something which I can't quite
Take out to the trash, but even if
I did take out what stinks so, it'd be
Sitting on the curb for over a week,
And then a neighbor would walk
By and wonder what kind of bad
The old bloke is trying to pull over
Though no one has the nerve, so
Far, to call the local sheriff to see
If someone else might move what
Seems so horribly wrong, right
There, but can't you see it, too,
It's right there, and I don't really
Have too much more time
With what seems so off as
The Brits sometime say when

Something isn't as fresh as it
Could be, but then, nothing
Quite appears anymore to be
Quite what it could be, does it?

Instructions on the Way Out the Door

Mother always reminded us as we opened
The front door, "remember who you are."
Now I wonder if I even know any more as
So many can no longer remember hardly
Anything, let alone who we might have been
And that's not before who we became after
That, and even worse, it's all going to not
Matter again and again as I've figured out
That when the door opens, in a new house,
In a new village, in a new century, that I
Can hardly remember who I was last night
Let alone this morning heading out so
Briskly into the bright light and late snow,
But did she know about all this was she
Just asking us to mind our manners, or
Remember that we were the preacher's
Kids and we'd better do right by that.
It's hard to know anymore, as the preacher
Is gone long buried in some park for the
Dead in some tiny little town in the South,
And of course, mother's on top, but both
Don't know that, but we do, and I suppose
That's all that matters, if anything matters
Especially as we step out into a new world
That looks a bit like yesterday, but so much
Of what was yesterday has just vanished
Into some grey part of what some call you.

III: Hello There

On Hearing Another Poet Has Died

I do not like dying at 72.
I simply do not want to.
But then, nobody wants to.
That's just it, some go, some stay.
I've never cared about any of this.
I can meditate for a few minutes,
But I'm not going to take a whole
Day to figure this one out. No sir.
I've just figured out the mystery
Of Adho Mukha Vrksasana. So
Why would I want to leave when
The asana is just now in the air.
It's a desire, of course, I know,
And desire brings us suffering,
I know, but I've kicked my old
Legs up the wall so many times
To come down without touching
The wall, that now, all I really
Want to do is float up to the
Wall, lift my shoulders, just
Like Pip might have, though
He had help with hanging
Like that, in the air, upside
Down. But I like the world
From upside down, who
Wouldn't, as it's such a blood
Rush, and of course, it doesn't
Last all that long, but long
Enough to try again maybe
Tomorrow. My dear wife
Asked just the other day,
What's the point of living
Like this, and she's in pain
Just every day, every hour,

71

And I'm just speechless
As to what to say, as no
Good argument can be
Made for saying, well,
There's time for something
You might want to do,
Maybe, but then, what
If we've all done what
We've ever wanted
To do, and that's so
Unimaginable, isn't it,
But some have thought
This through, not very
Well I might add, as now
They're not here to see
What might surprise
Anyone waking up into
New light, a new world,
But that's being a bit
Rosy about it, isn't it
As much of what's around
Here isn't rosy, isn't that
Right but still, there's
Coffee, and those egg
White wraps I've really
Got a taste for these
Days, so yes, I'm still
About to taste a few
Treats in the world,
And there's always
Scores of last night's
Games, and who doesn't
Like a game now and
Then, even if we're
Not out there, looking
Up into the night lights,
Holding the mitt even
If we're standing about

Ten feet maybe more
From where we should
Be standing, and that's
Sort of it, really, isn't
It, we're just not quite
Sure where we should
Be standing or maybe
We don't have to even
Be standing, as I've found
A long mat to be just
As good a place to
Send the arms or legs
Out into all sorts of
Odd directions, I should
Say, and who wouldn't
I mean, really, who wouldn't
Want to run through a
Sun salutation every
Day until the very end,
But it's so perplexing,
Don't you think so, as
To when the end is
Finally here, while some
Of our best friends are
Making sense of the long
Tube in some lab where
A lab tech says firmly
Lie still, but how do you
Lie still for 30 minutes
When the whole idea
Of being inside a missile
Is just too hard to put
Inside our heads, but then
The problem might be
In the head, or chest,
Or even an old leg
But not everybody is
In a tight squeeze as

Our friend is, so we
Might conjecture it's
Really something, more
Than that, it's a miracle
We're not yet in the
Missile, and that's
Quite wonderful, perhaps
Good enough reason
To pretend we're still
Here, looking for a cup
Of coffee, or whatever
Goes down nice and warm
In sips, and then, soon
It's all gone, and then
We start to wonder
What else, oh there's
The news, but I've been
Frightened of what's
Going to happen next,
So I've stopped reading
The news, and spend
More time figuring out
How to balance in such
A way, that the whole
Body is resting on the
Elbows, with a nose that
Close to the ground, so
You need to know what
In the world you are
Doing, as the ground
Is very close at this stage.
But isn't that what keeps
Us away from the ground
That we're all so close
But where was I oh
Yes, well, the rabbi last
Year made it perfectly
Clear, the purpose?

Really, it's just to live,
And not just to live,
But do something
But it's okay to just
Breathe, and really,
There are so many
New techniques for
Breathing, sometimes
Slow, sometimes fast,
Sometimes short,
Sometimes with a
Nostril closed, fingers
Folding in on all parts
Of a face, that heck,
We're all still glad
We have, not had.
What about you,
I'm pretty spent
Just getting us this
Far, so let's lie down
A bit, for a quick nap.

Please Stay

I'm here, okay, thinking you're here, though I know
You may not be here, as I don't see you or hear
Any whispers in the next room, or sense a cold
Chill when the room is already quite warm with
No sense of anybody, really, and that's what
I wonder about today, with you who as you know
Now, may not be here, but that's okay, when
You read this, you might be unless you're more
Finicky that I once thought as who would want
To be inside the mind of somebody's lines who
Takes you away from the misery you are already
In to something you'd never thought of even if
It's something you don't like, but that's the point,
Right, that we are here, linked like buds at least
For as long as you keep reading down the lines
But then what happens when you get to the
Bottom, and all you can muster is "say what?"
Or something cruel like that, who'd want to
Start up something, say a relationship with
Someone you've never known, not even by
Reputation, it's just that you saw what was
Going on here, and thought it might be swell
To go off on a spin, a brief delight, and see
What's here, even if, realizing toward the end
Of this, that's all there is, no big panorama to
Go "ahh" over but just the fact that you came
By and stayed for a minute or two, or even
Less than that which means so much and who
Hasn't said that too much around where you
Live as I've heard it said for just about anything
You could imagine, for admiring your outfit,
Your nails, your shoes, your inner you, your
Smile, your hee-haw laugh, the way you sip
Away on that very tall glass of Pinot as if

It's the last glass ever you're going to have
And somebody says right there that means
So much to me, but really, now you're asking
Where were we, well, we've really never even
Left, unlike all the friends you've walked away
From over the years, and all those troubles
That constantly wear you down, but now you're
Here, with me, hoping to god there's got to be
Some kind of meaning here, but what if there
Isn't any meaning, and then you start being
A bit defensive, saying things like it doesn't
Ever stop, or have inner rhyme, or why is it
Like this, but that's what we have to face isn't
It, that sometimes this is all we're going to
See, and we could go even further and say
As far as we can feel, but truly I have no idea
Where you are, but I'm glad you stopped by
Even if you stopped much further up, knowing
This is something not worth bothering about,
But that's okay, because I'm still here with
You, word by word, and hope you'll feel as
Joyous as I am now about what's here, now.

Spin Cycle

It isn't like you to say those things, like those things
You said just now, as I've not heard those things
But you seem quite interested, well, very interested
In saying those things to me and I wish I knew where
Some of that stuff was coming from as it's all new
To me like a cold fog blowing in a hurricane force
But that's you, isn't it, and I'm just something in
The way for all the blow to knock around a bit
But it's been that way, hasn't it, for how many
Years and sometimes I forgot how the big blow
Can just blow up such a big big storm in my head
Because that's usually where it goes, right up
There even though I don't want to let it go right
Up there as when it does, and when it does it's
Never something pleasant or interesting but more
The stuff of stuff I can't even begin to explain not
That I'd want to, oh for heaven's sake, no I wouldn't
But then that's what's going on, right, right now
Those words not just pouring out but blowing me
Right over as if I'm in some carnival whirly gig
Where the big tub starts whirling and whirling
And all of us are now gob smacked against the
Smooth metal that now feels like jet propulsion
Is pressing us into the shiny metal, and then, oh
Dear, none of us can move we're like butterflies
With no stick pins, can't move even the pinky
Finger and then o Jesus save us the floor starts
To drop right from under us and we're spinning
Faster and faster hair flying, if any of us have
Hair, skirts and shorts flying up but then no one
Can look down to see what's up as we're inside
Something that's spinning us around like the
Spin cycle, the last big fast one, in our new
Washing machine, yes, it's sort of like that,

That's what's going on in my poor brain as
Those things keep coming in spinning the
Poor brain cells around and around and
Around as if nobody has any sense of the
Kind of cellular damage that's going to happen
Unless someone, please someone, look for
The big black thick black cord that is keeping
All of us so electrified with our face skin
Just flapping and flapping around and the
Screaming is not loud at all no not at all
As nobody can ever scream when a mouth
Is just flapping and flapping it's a miracle
How somebody in there or say in me can
Even breathe but yes, that's what it is.

Don't Be Stupid

Stars are out there, many, everywhere, all the time.
Try not to think about this all the time.

Those stars, they're everywhere, even in us, all the time.
Don't be stupid about this. Try not to think about this all the time.

If it's important to you where Space ends, you may not
Be picking up the clothes you always drop on the floor,
For someone else to pick up. Learn to pick up, all the time.

Mountains change, rivers change, weather changes,
Volcanos are still erupting, it's colder some days.
Why is this so hard to understand? Don't think about it.

We can't remember everything that's happened. That's
Why we always mess things up. That's not hard, is it?

Don't be stupid. Another person is a person to appreciate.
You can't appreciate only those who look and act like you.
This isn't hard, but don't be so afraid. Take a deep breath.

Stop doing that. Whatever it is you are doing, stop that.
Why are you this old and you are still acting like that?
This isn't hard, it just takes practice. Don't think about it.

Of course, we are water. It goes in every day. We wash up.
We wash what's dirty. We are in awe of its beauty.
If you don't know that, wade in, go under, hold your breath.

Stop asking for applause. Do what you need to do well.
What's hard to understand about that? Are you still that needy?

The best line of that movie was Will it help? So stop worrying.
When has worrying every helped you to get things straight?

We are all here, standing in line. You can't make us go away
Like that. Stop blathering so. You look silly doing that.

Are you a busy person? Nothing to admire there.
Everything else in the cosmos is not busy, but it's there.
Staying busy will tire you out. Take a 2-minute time out.

Are you feeling any better? You know, there are no truths.
I know that's hard, but get used to it. Don't think about it
Ever again, just try doing everything you've done, better, that's
All.

Maureen's Gone and We'll Be Gone Soon, Too

Was it that she was so thoughtful, or
Courageous to last as long as anyone
Ever imagined anyone could or was it
Just dumb luck that some of us just stay
Around a bit longer than we should but
Way too many leave us speechless even
Before we hear the news like just yesterday
Somebody whispered Maureen's gone, too,
And how the heck weren't we told something.
She's gone just like that, out in the blue,
Or maybe up there, but definitely somewhere
But not here anymore which makes me even
More certain how disgusting this news is that
One of our friends just high tails it out of here
Like that, on a whim, even if the whim
Was a lingering growth or maybe even
A shrinking brain as it's way too hard
To get ahold of the coroner's reports
These days as they are guarded so care-
Fully in files no one really gives a hoot
About but maybe we do, and of course,
Of course, maybe we really don't want
To know all the deterioration our friend,
And all of your friends as well, had to
Endure for much too long perhaps there's
A better system, something like Soylent
Green, or something like that but even
If we tried that somebody just wouldn't
Want to say okay I'm good to go because
There's always something out there to
Do that we haven't done yet and who'd
Want to miss that, but then, we've missed
A lot of what we don't even know, right,

So maybe we should just take a slow deep
Breath and let it out like we did the other
Night when the lights were just about out.

On Awaiting Spring in Mid-January Long Before Dawn

It's still dark outside with light only seconds longer.
On Sunday we dip to single temperatures, with wind.
The grilled cod with pan vegetables recipe looked
So good, I looked around, then quietly tore it out.
The air is spitting ice, so few of us want to descend
All those steps as we might take flight, amused
At how light we are, then sadly, land on poured rock.
We sit in the right loge, mesmerized by the complaints
Of Wagner's soloists, sobbing for lost love of a sailor.
In the evening, we all bend over as far as we could
As it's a night of back bends, invigorating, breath taking.
A few intend to drive north, looking for hills to ski down.
Just yesterday I must have eaten over 30 plump blueberries.
In time our universe may implode inside another one.

No Plans

That's right, you're absolutely right, I'm not doing
Anything you might think important, I'm just here,
In this space, breathing lightly, touching the keys
Lightly, feeling light in the world, actually not
The world as I can't see past the walls of this
Little studio where I make worlds unlike the world
Out there, and of course you know what's out
There, don't you, but I'm not sure I care too much
More about what's out there, as finding what's
Here, or actually, up there, is something far more
Settling than settling into what actually is, isn't it?
So it's been like this for some time, and as the days
Seem even longer, and lines across the skin seem
Deeper, I wonder what was so important long
Ago that made me think doing something, anything
Was more important than doing something that
Amounted to nothing, but as a matter of fact, if
There is even an iota of a fact left around here,
As a matter of fact, I sense I'm moving closer
To not only not doing anything, but even a bit
More frightful, becoming less and less, lighter
And lighter, less of what I was, a bit emptier,
A bit more of what I've not yet found but that's
About all that's left, isn't it, rummaging around
For something else to do when thinking just
Yesterday isn't everything already almost done
And all that's left is what we haven't even
Seen hurling at us at light speed, that we'll
Be knocked down by such a fierce wind, but
Only if we wait a million or so light years
To come sweep us up, or by, or under, as
Someone just said, wait, wait, there's some
More we can do but maybe now it's not
As much fun as it used to be, when what
Was was more something than anything now.

So So Happiness

We can be so easily pleased, and so easily not, so
It's hard to know which might be more enjoyable,
Though who's going to volunteer here to wade
Through tons of this or that and barrels of details
Just so one of us can say, of course I'm happy.
Who's really happy here, that's what I'd like
To know and if that's so, how did anyone discover
What it is about the sheer loveliness of happiness
When so many of us wonder what is so lovely
About what so few find in their so unhappy lives.
This is what we need to discover, don't you
Think, for so many of us think if we can only
Find what so many want, then everything will
Be so much better if and when we can find
What so many think is so really wonderful
And special, though most of us know this
Will last only a few moments, and then we're
Wondering around trying to find what we
Lost, or perhaps even worse, what we never
Even had, but isn't this what we're always
Trying to find, or hold on to, or worse, keep
As it's such a pleasure to say, I'm so happy,
Aren't you, and if you aren't, what's wrong
With you, and that's what's holding so
Many of us up in tender limbo, isn't it,
That we have no chance at all of really
Feeling that tender moment that so many
Of us want to feel, yet so many of us
Are quite in utter despair longing so
For what none of us ever will know.
It's not that you have made all of us
So miserable, it's more that we have
So little clue as to how to climb out
Of what is so unexpected, a deep

Crevasse that some of us continue
To live wondering that's what everyone
Finds so normal, what everyone
Else is in, but then, we see you waving
And we want to find what you have
Even if we long for what we can
Never even imagine, even in the
Lonely world of which we always
Live in, despite our best intentions
Of loving you so much we're thinking
Maybe this is it, maybe this is all
We might ever want, a bit of what
You have, what everyone wants.

Nothing Matters

Of course, the news was bad when we heard nothing
Matters anymore, and most of us are so dadgum
Suspicious of reports like this as now and then, almost
All of us have had some brief moments of happiness,
But still we're stuck with this report that makes no
Sense to us, as we've passed through all sorts of states
Of bewilderment and absolutely hee-hawing moments
Of laughter, that it's just hard to take as anything more
Than some pothead spewing whatever crosses his
Brain pan, but the source of the news is troubling as it
Comes from very high up on the East Coast, and over
There, pretty much everyone knows what they're up
To even if it is just something that will pass like bad
Air that's choking just about all of us out here, but
Wouldn't you say it's troubling, sort of like living
Most of our lives as blisters popping and oozing out
The worst smell we'd ever put our nose to, so how
Could that really count, the one time we all saw
Something festering on our genitalia, or lips, or
Worse, somewhere in the behind area that no one
Can really see without getting out a bunch of mirrors
To see what in the heck is that burning in our butts
But just how can it be that all the stuff we've ever
Done, and some of it was pretty darn good, I'll add,
How can it all be for nothing as that pretty much
Says we're wasted here, we've been wasting pretty
Much all we've ever done, and you're wasted too,
And just how can that be that all the humans we've
Ever known, and then the billions we've never had
Time to meet, how can it be that we've turned into
Something that means we've all been fooling ourselves
Thinking that because we're here, because we're
Leaving such huge footprints just about everywhere
That even if what we do is just to take in whatever

Air is left, and whatever we can find even if it's
Brussel sprouts, boiling and baking and adding a
Few other unimaginable roots that might sustain
Us even for another hour, just how come this puttering
Around in the kitchen for anything to consume,
And of course, later, relieve ourselves near the
Few toilets that are left for all of us to use sometime,
Why is it that even this paltry little act of life doesn't
Add up to more than cold sprouts left on the stove?
This is, of course, very disappointing and most of us
Are just not going to take this news lightly, in fact,
I'm getting so steamed, so incensed, that we may
Have to just get on up there and at least stand
Outside the House and let somebody, anybody,
Know that there's a whole bunch of stuff that
Really does matter, doesn't it, doesn't it to you?

Just Before Spit Splatters All Over Your Face

Still here, and thanks for even wondering if I am though
Who in the heck out there wondered such a frightful
Thought, but I can certainly understand how someone,
Anyone, might come up with that as I've tried not to
Bother anybody with whatever I might be doing as
Nobody seems too interested these days in what so and
So is doing just the other day, and why hasn't anybody
Said something about so and so, even though everybody
Seems to be minding their very own business, though
It's a wonder, isn't it, that anybody is even talking nicely
To anyone these days, as there's so much flying spit
Travelling such short distances between two faces that
Obviously, no one, and I do mean no one, wants to get
Inside that spraying motion causing another commotion
By just being in there, between the two but isn't that
What most of us think we should be doing, as if the fire
Alarm is ringing right inside the heads of two spitfires
And someone, somebody thinks it's our business to
Go right in there with firehouses and spray everyone
Down with foam, but really, isn't there anything good
About spewing all over someone else over something
As stupid as oh my god my mistake please excuse me
And then the whole place is on fire as everybody wants
To swing and duck as it's so much more fun not being
Civil and polite but who cares if all the flying bodies
Landing on cracking backs start to buckle and by then
You can see, if you were still brave enough, that the
Floor we were on is making its own racket and soon
If not now some of us are beginning to fall right down
Into the next circle of rage where unbelievable dogs
Have opened up their canines and sending out such
A howl the likes none of us have heard, and all that,
All that business about a spilt glass of milk, okay,

It wasn't milk, but a fine tall stein of IPA or something
Delicious the other stout fellow was just about to
Drink in one big swallow, only somebody bumped
Him inside the noisy crowded hall and holy cow
It's almost as if the center of the world was going
To tip way way off its azimuth if there is such a
Thing holding us up or at least keeping us upright
For as long as possible until somebody, maybe even
A kind soul, comes along and sticks out a leg so we
Can trip over whatever is in front of us, and oh no
It's the big strapping whatever that is all red faced
And probably due for a whopping big stroke which
Is the last thing we need here, as he's going to
Take us all down, and who wants to go down, really?

Sun Burn

It seems that we've just about covered, or nearly covered
Just about all there is to cover, but then, I just know it,
Something is going to show up out of the blue, just like that,
And then we've got something we've never seen before,
Sort of like those visitors from way out in the universe
Somewhere, but they're good, they're very good as they've
Made us all forget we ever heard about that, but all of us
Know we've been covered up about that, or they were
Covered up, or some agency covered up, or somebody
Somewhere covered it all up, but by now we're all into
Something else, except nobody is taking the lead and pointing
To where we should all be headed by now, even though
It's late, very late, and unless we get started on where
We're supposed to get going, it's just going to get so much
Worse around here, as the air is a bit too stinky, and even
Some of the mountain tops have started to disappear and
Nothing like that has ever happened, no sir, nope, not ever,
Though things like this keep us dad gummed perplexed about
What's going to disappear next, like air or something huge
Like that, but then, our friends have disappeared, and where
The heck have they all gone to as it doesn't do any of us any
Good to go down to the cemetery and try to wake everybody
Up, as nobody, nobody is going to say get me out of here, now.
Nope, and it's like this, almost daily you could say, thinking
Something is here, like we've seen it forever, and then, poof,
It's just gone or something terrible like that, and it is terrible,
Wouldn't you say, or is that something you're just not ever
Going to talk about, but bugs of all kinds are just not here
Any more, and it's not like we liked them a lot, and we did
Not, but we always thought that bugs were here before us,
And they'd of course be here after the last of us takes leave,
But then, we don't really want to leave, but there's less and
Less of what's going to help us stay here, as the honey we
Used to just plaster on our toast is just about all gone.
Really, it's so hard to get around that idea, but I'll tell you

What, the big oceans are certainly not leaving us, in fact
They're pouring over us like never before with such son of
A bitch winds that like in one weekend, a whole island is
Under water, and so many who we knew and even spoke
To, they're gone too, so something is happening around
Here, and it's hard to get our old minds around this, but
Did you hear just the other day, all the ice up north is
Just gone, gone, and just where do you think it is now,
And nobody can get around that one yet, and I seriously
Doubt anybody will, though all sorts of ships are now sailing
Through what was 30 feet of solid ice, but see, that's what
I'm trying to tell you, something's going on, even though we
Still have a sunrise, just like in ancient times, but have you ever
Taken a look at how funny it's looked lately with all the clouds
Covering just about everything before the sun appears on what
We used to call our horizon, but even that seems to be changing,
And even true north has moved, and the trees down south,
They're all burning up so somebody else can plant soy beans, and
Soon, pretty soon, all the air over those soybeans, and I mean a
Million or more of them, well, they're just going to get scorched,
And that's just about the gist of it, we're all going to get scorched,
Though nobody, nobody knows when the whole place is going up.
Right?

Hello There

The elder of our tiny neighborhood cycled by just
In time for neither of us to know who said what
But then it doesn't really matter, does it, as we're
On our way to somewhere, but now that you ask,
I'm not even sure where we thought we were
Headed, but certainly headed somewhere, you
In your fancy white new outfit, me in a pair of
Dark pants and pink shirt, off to a meal to share
With someone, though we still don't know who
That might be, or how well the night will go.
But isn't that pretty much how it goes most
Of the time we set out on a drive to go somewhere
Even if we don't know exactly when we'll arrive,
Or even leave, or worse, not ever arriving back
Where we started this evening when the old
One down the road waved us by, and the
Two of us barely had enough time to look up
To see who it was that was kind enough to
Wish us a simple hello, but then, none of us
Expected to sit down on the curb and hear
About all the *tsuris* passing through each one
And for the most part, it's probably better
To just keep on moving, trying not to stop
To figure what in the world just happened
That will make our tiny lives even more
Miserable than they were yesterday, but
Somehow that's the pulse most of us have
These days, pushing the old misery back
As far as we humanly can, and hoping a
Friendly voice who doesn't expect anything
In return, lifts a voice that's barely there
Anymore as she pedals away on our old road
Lifting her wobbly arm once again, but now
She's fading into the end of day and then
You ask who was that Oh she's down the road

She lost her husband a few years ago even so
We see her fading away in the evening light
Almost gone, hearing in the distant something
With a wave and a sweet echo of Hello There.

Grey May

The sky is heavy. Soon we'll see a heavy
Downpour, and all of us will head down
The stairs, chasing all the new tiny streams.
This is not the May we wanted, even our
Poor forsythia looks so spiny with no blooms.
No one even thinks of opening the windows
For sunny May, and few say hello anyway.
Of course, we have a downtown, how silly
To ask, anyone can sit waiting for the bus
To take anyone anywhere, or over there.
Yes, the moon is out and nobody knows
Where it is, but sometimes after the rain
We see a painter's sky with clouds, then
Moon, then more clouds. Most of us
Walk to where we're going, but you
Are just passing through, asking about
Directions and weather far away from here.

All Aboard

How soon can I catch the train out of here?
No use catching the train out of here, is there?
What use is catching the train out of here
When all I want is to get out of here?
Somebody tell me what's the point of leaving
Like that, out of here, on the way to Santa Fe
Where I've never been except for one weekend.
Lovely isn't it, this situation where you see me
Just like this, trying to get out of Dodge in time?
Really, what's so important about leaving now
Instead of leaving long ago when I could leave?
Now it's pretty much impossible to leave as
I have no idea really where the train might stop.
You've been here, haven't you, wondering what's
Next, except you're a lot like me, not knowing
Really what might make the difference staying
And living through all of this, or not living through
All of this, and just to make it clear to those who
Are still here, it's something you've wondered
About, too, isn't it, so it isn't something that you're
Completely bamboozled by, is it, but then why
In the world did you stay where you are all these
Years, thinking staying was what would make
All the difference, but then what the heck makes
All the difference, yes? But then you're so wise
Much wiser than I'll ever be as I'm trying to find
Even a way out of the ever sinking situation
I'm in, but then, no one really cares about that,
Right and maybe that's the problem here, isn't
It, that all of us have no clue as to how to get
The heck out of here, and staying is just about
As worse, or is it, perhaps it's just another night
Wondering why has this turned out this way
As nobody ever nobody ever wanted things to

Turn this way, but they have old buddy, they
Have, and just exactly what are we going to do
About what's happened, and it's not that it has
Happened before, really, is that what you're
Thinking because if you are, well, we have a
Lot of work to do to get out of Dodge on the
Train that leaves late at night, and actually,
I'm a million miles from Dodge even though
I sat for years in the Long Branch Saloon
Wondering what might happen down the road
Next year, but now, it's been so many years
None of us have enough fingers to even count
What's happened to all of us, and then we were
So hopeful things would turn out so pleasant
And nobody ever told us about what the
Snipers were waiting for us high up in the trees
Of Vietnam, just waiting to sight in on those
Beautiful double brass bars that would almost
Instantly evaporate a squad who probably
Never ever wanted to be here, or there, but
Then we were, and so maybe that's how all
Of this probably started, like that, like now,
And we're pretty close to losing it, but then,
We're standing at the end of the line just
About to board the train for somewhere
Out of here, and please, please, would
Someone just say where we might last
The long night sitting on that seat, staring
Out into the darkness just like we did
When our whole firebase was overrun?
Please, who knows a good place to step
Off the world and enter into something
Nobody ever expected, like this, now.

So What Do You Do?

Something, that's about what it seems, at least
For now, maybe. It's a bit like someone saying
What do you do? To be honest with you, and
I'm not always as honest as I'd like, I'm still
Wondering about that, the what do you do
Thing. It's always something, wouldn't you
Say? There's never been a not doing, but
Lately, that seems indeed pleasurable over
Piles of laundry and late bills. Is that what
It all comes down to, doing something,
Somewhere, sometime, somehow? Would
You ask a Paleolithic hunter the same?
He and/or she is just hungry and all the
Dinner animals are either skittery or way
Too big to bring down. Every day has a
Certain melody, sometimes operatic, but
Often, just a sweet song someone hums
Now and then, though lately, more blues
That makes both of us just want to lie
Down and die. But, thank heavens, we
Don't as we want to keep listening, even
A little, just to see what tomorrow might
Bring. Isn't everyone wondering about
Tomorrow? Or hoping for tomorrow?
Some have already dropped dead from
Not knowing about what to do next, but
For others, maybe you, we're already
Dreaming way ahead of where we already
Are. It's also very possible none of us
Really know what we're doing, or what
We've done, or haven't done, or don't
Even know what we should have done.
But like a miracle everyone here keeps
On doing as that's why we're here, just

To do something. Of course that's right,
And even if you're not doing, your old
Brain on life support is still scanning
The universe for what's in front of us,
Wondering, of course, how soon we'll
Not even have those electrical hot wires
As the way this works out is we don't
Get to do this very long, even though
Everyone thinks this certainly could go
On, like forever, and then, forever is
Already over, and there you are either
In a tiny box of bones and ashes, or worse,
Just lying like that down below not doing
Anything again, ever, anymore, anywhere.

The End

This is the title to the end, but you're nosy
Enough to want to know end to what, but
Isn't that obvious by now, haven't you
Been keeping up with your busy busies?
Don't tell me you couldn't read through
The lines and predict the massive fallout
That took place possibly so long ago no
One really can comprehend something
Way way back so very far back but then
How did it last so long, that's truly the
Mystery here, and nobody really knows
That either, in fact nobody knows anything
Around here anymore, just a huge grey
Funk hanging over us, not unlike fog but
With fog it always smells fresh and cool
And this doesn't have that feeling, no
Not at all, rather bad heartburn, eye
Aches, if one can call it that, of course
The migraines are coming in on a daily
Basis knocking the wind out of all of us
But then we've read the literature about
All of that, and that's certainly partly
A way to say, so it was that, but nobody
Really knows what that was that came
Through like some night rider on a black
Horse tiptoeing into town so not even
The flying bugs circling around us had
Any sense there was going to be one
Very big doom coming through and
Nobody, I mean nobody, really had any
Training for something like that, but
Who does in end times like these, who
Really does, who expects something
Like this to come down from on high
Like that scaring the b'Jeezus out of

All of us, and some of us have already
Lost their sight, and some can't even
Speak about it, and good Lord, some
Don't even have limbs anymore, so
Yes it turned out to be very bad, as
In worse case bad, as in nothing we've
Ever seen around here could ever
Have been as bad as that, but it was.

Keep Talking, Everybody, Keep Talking

In the end, we don't know too much, do we?
Of course, a few can read aloud, and even write
Something that might be helpful to the rest of us.
But we chatter along just like all the sparrows
Twittering in the bushes, busy with nit-picking,
Or worse, sounding chirps of worry and alarm
For the big birds which have killer instinct eyes.
Then we have to recognize all those who so
Carefully wrote something down for someone
Else, but who remembers it all, that's what's
So hard to bend and fold neatly into a brain.
Have we forgotten anything? Most everything.
Personally, I no longer remember Miss Neblong's
Long butt weathered paddle she used on us
And so many other frightened to death urchins,
But we're here, and probably not obsessing over
Third grade nightmares that keep a few awake
Even now. But walk into any library, even the
Old book stalls in Alexandria, if anyone is able.
Or you might remember stumbling through
As a grade schooler, or even your old college
Building that housed huge numbers of so
Many impossibly difficult tomes read only
Under threat of a quickly diminishing final
Grade, but then, nobody really worries about
Such things anymore, in fact, it's really hard
To figure just exactly what is worrying almost
Everyone these days, and it's not always the
Little kid just about to step off the curb who's
Pulled back from the brink by an angry you-
know-who. So we have good data on all those
Who continue to blather and babble until
Most of us are almost crying, or bursting
A blood vessel somewhere inside of us but
We really couldn't say exactly where, could

We? That's the problem, we hardly know
Anything that's useful, but we're babbling
And blathering (see line 32 ff.) over so much
And most of us assume we are smarty-pants
Just because some neurons way up there
Have triggered some incomprehensible string
Of syllables and morphemes that makes us
Sound as if we do know what we're talking
About, but we don't, do we? So what's
There to do about this conundrum that never
Stops to think for just a minute, as we have no
Idea what's really going on, and even those
With all the liquid assets in the world, even
Those with gold plated toilet seats, surely
They know about as much as we did back in Miss
you-know-who's grade school class just before
The butt warmed paddle comes out once again
To frighten us from now until kingdom come.
Of course, it's your turn now, and I can even see
You're not listening a hoot to any of this, but instead
Preparing a long and tedious yakety-yak about how
All of this is balderdash, as nobody really thinks
This way, and it's very possible, very, that when
We all lay down after a busy yapping and yawning
Day, we'll all wake up, you hope, ready or not
To go at it again without even a pittance of memory
For any of this business, but I just wanted you to
Know, we're all in some kind of loop, and we'll go
On and on about this until somebody, somewhere
Kicks up a dust storm about all this, but then, if that
Happens, most of us, as planned, will already be dust.

Soon

These are the last days, or at least
We suspect so, as all have passed
Through another distilled moment,
Though how many more do we have
As that's not clear to any of us, but
Think about it for a moment, please
As soon, perhaps not so soon, we'll
Not have any more time, and who here,
Or you, just glancing at this, doesn't
Want more of that, but then, some of us
Are so beyond our expiration date,
So we'd hope they'll go quickly, but
Not in any queue, and certainly not
At the same morgue, or whatever
Last cold bed might be waiting, but
Then as for the rest of us, we'll all
Have to wait our turn, won't we, and
Of course some want to completely
Ignore what's just around the corner,
And others have seen a hearse appear
Over and over either in their dreams
Alone at night, or just slipping into
Daydreams if anyone has time for
That sort of play, but so many of us
Just don't know, do we? And none
Of us look forward to that time, but
For many, it's been quite wonderful,
Yet for others it's a long nightmare
And who'd want that forever and
Ever for so brief a time here, where
We are, and as well, where we're not.

How Long?

The ride has always been something else, seldom
Something not, sometimes provocative, but really,
Some of the bones and bruises are starting to push
Through, and as expected, the brain is probably
Shrinking, but thank heavens I didn't reserve a
Plated box lowered down far enough from wolves
And hungry bears. The snow isn't even snow today
As its just spitting, even melting in the eyes, so
Sniffing isn't probably recommended as most of it
Will just settle in the gut only to make more
Dripping snot when it's so wet and icy out.
Mother was always asking when she would die,
As if anyone knew anything about expiration dates
For the dead, but she was the middle child and
Why was she alive when all the younger kids,
And even all the older sibs, were now resting,
Planted somewhere in the South where plastic
Flowers always bloom on *yahrzeits* even if none
Had ever heard of such annual events. So here
I'm perched on a high chair, coffee and croissant
On a high table, looking out at busy bodies
On their way to their next adventure, or maybe
Just forgotten milk or eggs. I wouldn't mind at
All making an exit here though it would be
So unsettling for all around as two pre-teens
Giggle over vids on their brand-new phones,
Another is pouring over a philosophy textbook,
Probably required, both hands holding the head
To better absorb all the dense nonsense, then looking
Up, looking sad, looking out at the grey afternoon.
They might enjoy the novelty, for who wouldn't
Want to talk about what happened right next
To where we were? There'd be a handful of
Well wishers, but in another hundred years, whose
going to remember any of this as who can recall

Even last year? Of course I feel fine, but then
One day, all of us are not going to feel so fine.
Even the fading tulips I just brought home, now
They are all drooping terribly, blooms bowing
On the outside of that lovely green vase
Where tulips and daffs always look so fine.
Outside, the snow continues to drip, with
Spring only four more years away for some
Of us, and some, as you know, will not see
Spring arriving with daffs and tulips on the
Lawn, but placed in parks all across well
Manicured lawns where stones tell us, if
We are curious, where somebody still is.

Just Wait

Forget serenity, contentment, bliss, joy, even a
Happy happy, or a calm beating heart, for out
Here, it's miserably cold, and no one is opening
A door with a come on in, warm yourself up,
How about a cup of warm tomato soup, but
Instead, the pit bull straining to chomp all the
Way through to the shin is so much more
An existential angst, and the trick is not to let
The master with the leash think for even a second
You're the least bit disturbed with facing a big
Pit amputation. Of course, the walk home at dusk
And opening the creaky door might open into
Some sense of safety from the winds that break
Even frozen eyelashes, fingers numb, even with
Mittens, so clearly, it's pointless to pick up anything
That might be of any interest even if what's there
Is only a few feet away, and so, it's like this every
Day, but it's really not that cold out, and the pit
Bull is just a yappy chihuahua, and the door that
Leads to safety, well, let's just completely forget
That as that comfort left so long ago. So this is
What we face. Of course, you don't think anything
Ever even close to this will happen to you, how
Could you, but just wait, those sunny days, warm
Sandy beaches, a lovely person next to you who
Wants to bathe you in kisses just about everywhere
So just wait, you'll see, even when you only wonder
Why all around you has suddenly turned quite
Chilly, and then an iceberg floats by with a thin
As bones Polar bear who stares at just you, though
What you see can't even move to swim all the
Way to you, and eat in exasperation what
You'd call you, but no need to worry, just wait.

Last Wishes

Let them plow me into the fields.
Let me drift as ash in the blue sky.
Let me not be prayed over all night.
Just drag me across the ocean floor
So I can provide food
For all the tiny crustaceans.
Let me become food for all.
Come feast with me.
Let the crows gnaw on fresh eyes.
Let the little four-footed creatures
Sniff and feed all their way through who I was.
Then let the maggots and bugs join in.
Then let the Sun bake my bones.
So we're clear, then, no box, no silk,
No *Yitgadal*, no tears, no standing
Around wondering what's for lunch.
No distilling what now is Not.

DeWitt Clinton is Professor Emeritus at the University of Wisconsin—Whitewater, and lives in The Village of Shorewood, Wisconsin. His four collections of poetry include *The Conquistador Dog Texts, The Coyot. Inca Texts,* (New Rivers Press), *At the End of the War* (Kelsay Books, 2018) and *By A Lake Near A Moon: Fishing with the Chinese Masters* (Is A Rose Press, 2020). He is a student of Iyengar Yoga, and occasionally substitutes as a yoga instructor for seniors in The Village of Shorewood.

Made in United States
North Haven, CT
13 November 2021

11110792R00067